SALES SIMPLIFIED:
Tools, Techniques and Tips to Increase Revenue

Author: Gail Zelitzky

Book Design & Illustrations: Elizabeth Scott

Copyright 2020 Silver-Robins Consulting LLC

ISBN: 978-0-9891223-7-5 EBook

ISBN: 978-0-9891223-6-8 Print

TABLE OF CONTENTS

Are you ready to stand in your own power and smash your sales record out of the park? Do you fervently believe that when you are in business, you are in sales?

In business ABSOLUTELY NOTHING HAPPENS UNTIL THE CASH REGISTER RINGS!

If you are truly open to achieving the success you've dreamed about, hang on because we are going for a ride.

Erase everything you know about selling. This book is out to change your perspective and fill your mind with new ways of thinking. Whatever you've thought about sales before, forget it. Effective selling is no more, and no less, than gaining people's trust.

Does this describe you?

"People like me; they believe in what I sell. My service makes a difference in their lives. They buy from me because they know I deeply care about their outcomes."

Do you know, with certainty, that they feel this way about you? If not, we have some work to do! Once people like you, you gain their trust and they believe in your knowledge, offer them options that solve their challenges and provide a way for them to work with you.

I began to understand the psyche of selling when I franchised 300+ independent retail liquor stores nationwide. Most of the stores operated under the same name, FOREMOST™ Liquor Stores—PAY LESS…*Get More at Your Foremost Liquor Store™*; had equal access to marketing, a co-op advertising program, sales promotions, in-store merchandising, co-op buying and operations consulting; and, still, their performance was all over the place. Many languished between $250,000 and $2 million a year. A number of the stores never reached 1 million dollars in sales. However, the top revenue producers did $6, $8, $12, $15 million a year in annual sales. Today, those same stores bring in sales of $60-100 million dollars a year.

My life-long career to understand the psychology of success and how it can be applied to the science of selling, began back then. My quest to understand how the successful think, and why there exists such a success disparity among business owners, has been a life-long pursuit.

Business owners who pour their hearts into making others' lives easier, deserve to enjoy bottom-line profitability. They should achieve their goals and live the lives they desire. Solid profit allows them to positively impact their employees' lives.

For 18 years now, I've sustained a highly successful coaching business providing consulting services for success-driven entrepreneurs.

At the core of this success is my belief that sales are the lifeblood of your business. Revenue drives every aspect of your growth. Without enough sales, your marketing suffers, inventory declines, you can't hire the right people or network in the right places. You never gain the influence that comes with power. In other words, your personal and professional growth is hampered. Even if you are a sole provider or solo professional, without enough sales, success in all areas of your life will elude you.

The good news is everyone can learn to sell. With the proper system, insight and techniques, you are armed to educate every prospect to see why they need your product or service, answer all their objections and close the sale.

Selling should be fun. If you are to appreciate the 'thrill of the kill', you must commit to being the best you can be. We are not talking about notches on your business license. We are talking about how thrilling success is. Passion sells! Knowledge sells! And, mastery of the sales process sells! No one wants to buy from an inept salesperson.

This statue was a gift from my father after I joined his company. He was impressed with my selling skills.

It's no secret I've been selling my entire life: first, it was getting buyers for the lemonade I sold on a makeshift stand on hot, muggy Chicago summer afternoons. Later, it was advertisers for the school paper and Moms to make costumes for the school plays. I didn't understand then that influence was on my side and I had natural persuasive powers.

During my years at Foremost Sales Promotions, Inc., franchisor of Foremost Liquor Stores, I sold co-op advertising to distilleries, wineries, breweries, distributors and importers to merchandise the stores and run newspaper ads. We created unique sales promotions that brought customers in and gave us the reputation as trend-setters.

In my next business, Liquor by Wire / Liquor.com, I parlayed those relationships into advertising support for the award winning marketing tools we created that drove our business growth and catapulted us to 4 million dollars in just a few years.

Early on I understood that selling is quite simply understanding the needs of your customers, creating a plan and working it. Once you develop the structure, it fits neatly into a framework that can be managed day after day.

When I became a consultant, I created a proprietary system called Think Sales so my clients could apply it to their businesses and SOAR. The biggest challenge my clients face is making time to sell. When you consider that Sales is one of the 4 pillars that drives growth, there is no choice but to construct a system and maximize every moment.

If you own your business, you are the ultimate rainmaker for your company. You are the role model for your employees. With the right culture in place, everyone who works for you sells for you, regardless of their job description.

This book is dedicated to your success. I hope it enables you to shift how you think about sales and provides you with the tools and techniques you need to become more confident and be the best revenue generator.

If I can help you clarify the process further, please do reach out. Business is dynamic, complex and ever-changing. Each stage requires different skillsets for both the business and the leader to continue to grow. My goal for you is to scale quickly and maintain long-term sustainability.

My mission for you is to Think Sales and Grow!

GAIL ZELITZKY

773-957-8582
www.GailZelitzky.com
Gail@GailZelitzky.com

CHAPTER ONE:
DE-MYSTIFYING SELLING

THE THINK SALES™ SYSTEM

"Plan your work and work your plan."

Behind every successful sales person is a system.
Systems and Process are the foundation of your business - twin drivers that form the backbone of your sales system and allow you to grow. Real leaders accept they don't know everything. They know their egos must be checked at the door.

Selling, itself, is a professional pursuit and, happily, almost anyone can learn it. If you truly wish to increase your sales skills you must be willing to read books on selling, listen to podcasts, watch videos and attend sales seminars. If your business is to continue growing, you can never stop learning.

If you truly wish to increase your sales skills, you must be willing to follow a system and continuously upgrade your skills. Consistency is crucial. The goal is to Think Sales from the core of your existence, achieve the performance you expect and, above all, turn your customers' dreams into reality.

Once you gain strength in selling, adapt what you learn to your own unique style. Nobody feels about your business the way that you do. Keep passion in your back pocket.

Remember, you are the heart of your company. Your success is a direct result of:
1. Knowing the attitudes and values that drive you.
2. Knowing what makes you a market leader.
3. Knowing your team and how well you communicate what you value.

The Think Sales System
1. Plan
2. Prepare to Sell
3. Sell
4. Close the Sale

Knowledge and mastery of the sales process are the keys to successful selling. Into this you create the system and that becomes your plan.

As you go through this book you will find all the tools you need to follow these steps.

A SELF-ASSESSMENT

Let's start by taking this self-assessment:
(Rate yourself on a 1-10 scale: 10 being excellent, 1 being poor)

A Self-Assessment
Do you have a sales system?
How closely do you follow it?
How well do you understand the needs of your prospect?
How prepared are you each time you meet a prospect?
What is your closing rate?
What do you think of your overall sales skills?
Do you ask for feedback?
Do you have a follow-up process?
Do you know how to maximize each sale?
How committed to success are you, really?

Highlight all the areas that are 6 or below. You can dive into the chapters that tackle those challenges first. While it's best to read the book from front to back, learn the skills that will bring you the fastest return. Then go back and review the others.

HOW MUCH ARE YOU WORTH?

You are in business to be profitable. The products and services you sell are your path to profit. If you hope to support yourself well, enable your employees to make a good living, and, give back to your world, you must be successful. How much money do you want to earn?

Yearly Income (50 weeks)	Weekly Salary (40 hours)	Hourly Rate
$200,000	$4,000	$100.00
$225,000	$4,500	$112.50
$250,000	$5,000	$125.00
$275,000	$5,500	$137.50
$300,000	$6,000	$150.00

If your time is worth $150 per hour, are the sales you make reflecting your earnings potential? Want to earn 6 figures or more? Provide value that warrants the price you charge.

THE MATHEMATICAL APPROACH

Numbers drive every aspect of your business. Without the proper metrics in place, so you can clearly understand your numbers, you sell yourself short. You make growing your business harder than it has to be. I've taught entrepreneurs in every stage of business. When we discuss finance and the financial implications of how they price their products and services, and what it takes to get each sale, it is common for them to experience giant AHAs and run to replace their accountants and CFOs. They suddenly realize that the information that helps them grow faster has always been available but they never accessed it properly.

Selling is exactly the same. Ask yourself these questions.

1. How many appointments (phone or in-person) must you make to reach your sales goal?
   Weekly _____ Monthly _____ Quarterly _____
   How much time do you spend making that many calls? #hrs____

2. Do you break sales down into different size deals? How many and what sizes?
   Small _____ Medium _____ Large _____

3. How long is your sales cycle?
   ☐ Immediate
   ☐ 90 days
   ☐ 120 days
   ☐ 365 days
   Do you consider this when setting fees? Yes___ No___

4. What else do you need to know to make a realistic plan? _____
   _____
   _____
   _____

Whether your revenue comes from one gigantic $10 million sale or hundreds of $100 sales, there is a direct ratio between contact and closing. A sales dashboard provides you the information you need to sell smarter.

If you put in too much time prospecting, and don't get enough sales, it's time to find a new approach. Maybe you should hire a leads provider and only spend your time meeting qualified prospects?

What are the metrics that drive your business? Is it number of sales a day, a month, a year? Maybe it's the number of clients - new clients, retained clients, lost clients. Is it the size of the deal?

This simple dashboard is easily constructed to review the metrics that drive your business on a monthly basis. Set a goal for each month, then track the results.

Your Objectives	$ Revenue	# Sales	# New Clients	# Retained Clients	Small Medium Large
January					
February					
March					
April					
May					
June					
July					
August					
September					
October					
November					
December					

CHAPTER TWO:
PREPARING TO SELL

GET CLEAR ON STRATEGY

Peter Vaill, professor of Human Systems at George Washington University:

"It's like living in permanent white water where problems change as fast as solutions are developed. What worked yesterday may not work today and tomorrow may bring even more change. To stay in the game, you need a strategic plan positioning yourself in the marketplace. This means knowing what you have to sell, who needs it, how it provides value to customers and how to differentiate it, and yourself, from the competition."

Its time to write down the overall strategies you will use to inspire growth. These are not tactical, but broad strokes that provide clarity to your everyday work. In terms of sales, they might include:

1. Revise website to draw in more viewers who seek information on our products/ services.
2. Draw up a sales plan.
3. Revisit Groups, Networks and Organizations in which we network and serve on boards.
4. Realign our thinking to better serve our customers' needs.
5. Design workshops to attract new clients.
6. Upgrade our approach to social media, podcasts and video.

Now, define your own strategies to make sales soar.

1. _____

2. _____

3. _____

4. _____

5. _____

6. _____

Once you know the strategies, turn this information into an action plan that provides the tactical steps required to achieve your goals. For each strategy delineate the everyday work.

- What is the goal?
- What are the steps to take?
- Who will be responsible?
- What are the measures of success?
- What are the financial implications?
- What is the deadline for completion?

It might look like this:

Goals	Action Steps	Who is Responsible	Measure of Success	Financial Implication (+ or -)	Deadline

This roadmap takes all the thought out of "What will I do today? and insures you and your staff are as productive each day as possible.

CREATE SMART GOALS

When determining your goals, make sure they pass the Smart Test:

SMART TEST

S   Specific: results you expect

M   Measureable: quantifiable

A   Achievable: fit sales ability, and current or expected market conditions

R   Realistic: not too easy or too hard

T   Time-based: when it will be accomplished

Create no more than 6- 8 goals each year for each area. These may include sales, marketing, human and capital resources, technology and financial goals.

Revenue, or sales goals should be set new each year after reviewing previous year's results.

TRACK RESULTS MONTHLY

For best results, track sales monthly. Tracking sales provides insight into which products/services are most popular and at what price points. If there are other sales team members, each should track their goals as well. When setting goals, consider: How much business did we do last year? How much business was from existing clients? How much business was from new clients? What increases are realistic to expect this year?

Your Objectives	Sales Goal	Actual Sales	Average Sale	# New Accounts	# Exisiting Accounts
ANNUAL					
January					
February					
March					
April					
May					
June					
July					
August					
September					
October					
November					
December					

If you consistently make your monthly goals, increase the goal. If you consistently miss the monthly goal, brainstorm with your team why this may be happening. Reduce the goal if it is unrealistic. Hold a creative brainstorming session in which you ask: "What are all the ways we can better reach new and existing customers?"

WORK THE PLAN

Any plan is only as good as the person who works it. You can set all the goals you want but if you do not take them seriously, you can't expect the plan to work. That is why tracking results monthly is so crucial to success. When you stay on top of the results you have an opportunity to course-correct. In fast-moving times, you can't afford to review numbers once a year, or quarterly. Changes have to be made in the moment to alter the results. With sales, every day lost affects your bottom line. (Are you receiving timely financials with the data you need to review each month?)

Ask yourself, every single day:
What do I have to do today *to keep on target?*

If you have employees, make sure to set goals together and review them monthly. This is something you can't put off because it directly affects your bottom line. Equally important is to make time to coach your sales team and keep them apprised of any new developments that affect what they sell. At the end of each day, revisit your plan.

Ask yourself:
- *What did I accomplish today?*
- *What will I continue to do more of tomorrow?*
- *What will I continue to do less of tomorrow?*

And then, get back out there, and sell!

CHAPTER THREE:
SELLING IN BUSINESS DEVELOPMENT MODE

YOUR PERSONAL STYLE CONTRIBUTES TO YOUR SUCCESS
Let's seriously consider why anyone should buy from you.

1. Does your personal image support the types of products and services you sell? ☐ Yes ☐ No

2. How and what do you offer that is something special? _____
   _____

3. How do your products/services benefit customers over your competitors?_____
   _____

4. What problems could the customer have by not using your products/services?
   _____

5. How can you out-serve your competitors' services? _____
   _____

6. What support or added value can you offer your customers? _____
   _____

This is not easy to grasp. Who you are, why you sell the products/services you sell, and how you sell them fully determines your success. We've all met Arrogant Al, Debbie Downer, Self-satisfied Susie and Messy Mavis. We've also experienced Authentic Adam, Realistic Ruth, Helpful Hermione and Problem-solver Pete. Who would you rather do business with?

I'm constantly amazed by people who simply are not tuned in to the affect they have on others. This is a book on sales, but I urge you to take a course on Emotional Intelligence. If you are not getting the results you seek, consider how you interact with people.

KNOW YOUR TARGET MARKET
You must understand the problems that plague your market - you are the solution and your prospects can't wait to find you.

Ask yourself, what are 3 distinctive things we do that are above and beyond our customers' expectations? Write them here:

1. _____

2. _____

3. _____

Power comes from knowing who your perfect client is, how you will reach them and what to say to them. How well do you identify with your market? Are you intimately knowledgeable about your potential customers? Does your call to action result in an immediate response and desire for the products/services you offer? This is key to your growth. Selling when there is no need or desire for your products/services is a waste of your time. When desire exists you are not selling! You are providing an answer to someone's problem.

First determine if you are selling business to business, business to customer or business to government?

Fill in the blanks:

1. Describe your geographic target market – where do your customers live?_____

_____

_____

_____

2. Describe the demographics of your target market – what generation are they, how and where do they live, what is important to them? _____

_____

_____

_____

3. What stage of business are they in? _____

_____

4. What is their income level, education attainment? _____

_____

5. What do they do in their spare time? _____

_____

6. Describe your association target market(s) – what organizations do your customers belong to, what conferences and trade shows do they attend? _____

_____

Once you know your target, your job is to determine where you fit? Are you selling luxury, high-end products or price sensitive, low-end products? Do you specialize in custom, feature-driven products or mass-production? Which of the value disciplines do you excel in:

- Customer Intimacy - you center on delivering superior customer value.
- Operational Excellence - you value price and convenience and center on cost reduction, competitive pricing and ease.
- Product Leadership - you work to be creative, get to market quickly, be relentless in your quest to solve unknown problems.

What is YOUR primary Value Discipline? _____

_____

PROSPECTING

Just as there are fish everywhere in a lake, likewise, in sales, prospects can be found in lots of places. Everyone you meet is a likely prospect. But defining who your target market is – who will absolutely buy your products or services, is the most important work you have to do. Once you know that, spending time in front of prospects produces greater payoff.

Mapping out who your prospects are, and where you can find them, directs your efforts.

Consider this diagram. Often we overlook the most obvious connections. Prospect sources are everywhere in your social, familial or collegial sphere. I'll bet many people in your circles don't have the slightest idea of what you do for a living. We can't wait for them to ask. When your belief about what you do is strong and passionate, it is up to you to educate them. Sometimes you'll derive direct business from them. Other times they become referral sources and alliances. When you believe that your product or service is of real value to your circles, then you can't help talking about what you do and how you help your clients. It's okay to bring this up in ordinary conversation. I am not suggesting you bombard people with constant information. I am suggesting you remain alert to opportunities.

[See diagram, next page]

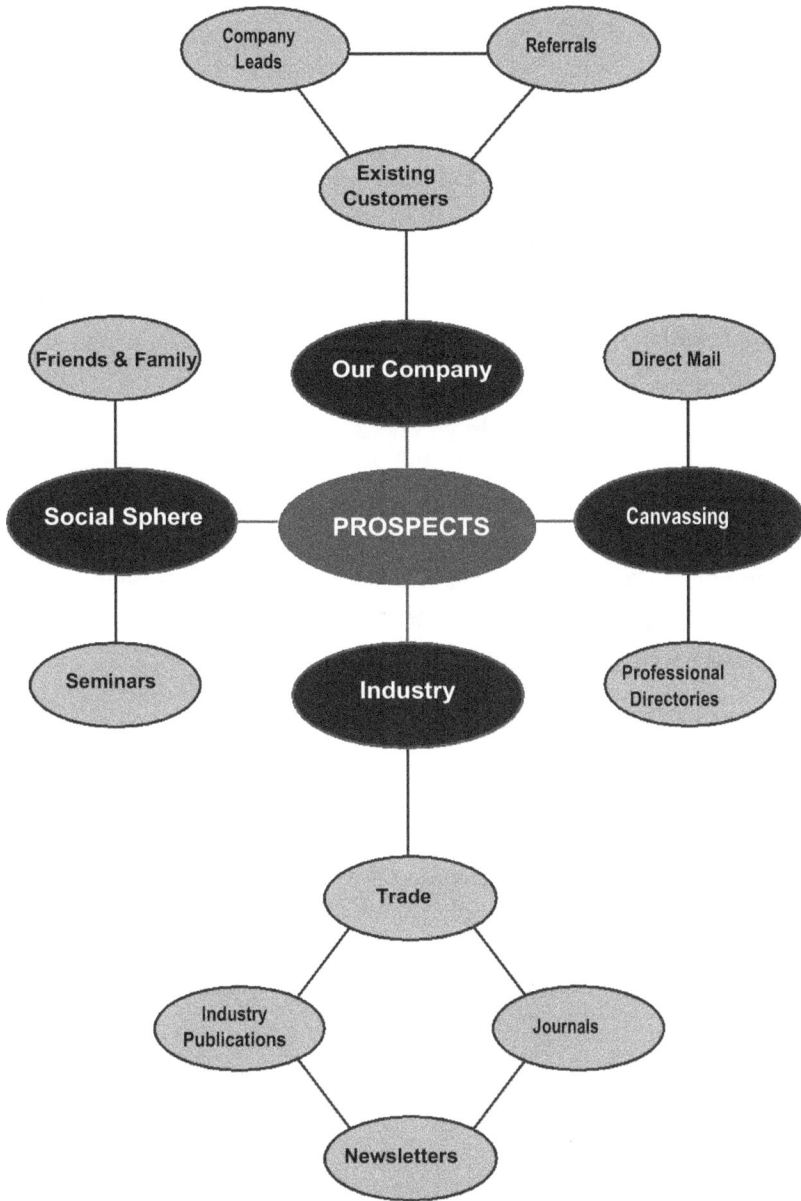

Look at this chart. Make it your own. Add names of people you know beside each category. Search LinkedIn to find people in the industries you want to sell and get introductions. Some people require personal phone calls, others will connect by email. Some use Instant Messenger. Others need to be met at events. Don't overlook any opportunity. Make a list and set appointments.

DEVELOP YOUR SALES PLAN

Since selling is all about building relationships, crafting a business development strategy is key to your growth. Networking is at the top of the list. Networking means connecting with a selected group of people who may be able to use your products/services, help you with resources or referrals, and who you may be able to help with resources or referrals.

Why Network?

- To meet people and turn them into customers/clients.
- To build and nurture long-term relationships.
- To know people who can help you help your clients.

When networking properly, no one feels pressured, used, or put on the spot. You may get direct business from people you meet or you may get indirect business from them through referrals. Networking is a process whereby over time you develop trust with the people you meet. Networking takes time (generally 5 hours weekly preparing for and attending events) and is measurable.

Prospecting for sales isn't just something you do once in a while or whenever you're feeling panicked for new business. On the contrary, it is an effective marketing tool—an essential part of your arsenal—that you must do all the time.

Before attending any event, prepare yourself.

- What is your purpose in attending?
- How are you going to introduce yourself?
- What do you want to know about the people you meet?

Oh, The Places You'll Go

Take the time to create a written prospecting plan that includes networking. Think about the places you go and the people you meet. Do they fit your target market? Do they have potential for providing referrals and resources? How can you leverage these relationships once you develop them? Plan your time productively and you will achieve results.

Develop your networking plan by answering these questions:

1. What are your networking goals? *(Remember every plan needs measures to track)*
   _____

   a. How many events will you attend each month? _____
   b. How many prospects and warm relationships do you hope to meet? _____
   c. How much marketing dollars will you allocate for this? Include annual
      membership costs, event fees, coffee dates, etc. _____

2. Where do you network currently? *(Have you tracked the results you achieved in the past year to make sure it is worthwhile to continue?)* _____
   _____

3. Where do your "key" customers/clients network? _____
   _____

4. How much time can you realistically devote to networking? Plot out the time you
   will spend on a calendar and see if it is feasible. _____
   _____

5. What two organizations should you consider joining? _____
   _____

6. What should you do more of in the coming year? _____
   _____

7. What should you do less of in the coming year? _____
   _____

8. What else do you need to do/learn to become an even better networker? _____
   _____

9. Who can you learn it from? _____
   _____

10. How will you follow-up? *(Remember to leave time on your calendar to follow up with all the people you will meet. You must do this within 48 hours or the time spent will be wasted. People will forget you existed!)* _____

Now take all of this information and create your Sales Plan.

Sales Plan
Every plan demands you focus squarely on revenue and client acquisition.

Goals: New Revenue $_____   #New Clients _____

My Target Market _____

The prospect meetings I hope to make. Include Name, Company and Contact
information: _____
_____
_____

Places to Network _____
_____
_____

Follow-Up Plan _____
_____
_____

Let's not forget about your employees. Companies that engage every one of
their employees in the sales process find their employees help drive growth.
Consider these suggestions to empower your staff to sell for you.
- Recognize your employees' spheres of influence.
- Encourage your employees to network on your behalf.
- Train your employees to communicate your message.
- Teach them to properly network and dress appropriately.
- Provide each and every employee with business cards imprinted
  with their names. (Yes, every one!)
- Train them to target prospects and work a room.
- Help them by practicing role-playing.

If you do not feel capable to engage your team yourself, hire a coach to help
you through the process.

Whatever you do, the important thing is to do it and get the business!

INTRODUCE YOURSELF MEMORABLY.

Once you have a complete description of all the potential buyers for your products/ services, you are ready to tailor your introduction to make an impact. The most important one-moment in your life is your 'elevator speech'. It is an opportunity to create interest. When networking or introducing yourself at an event, the most difficult question to answer is always "What do you do?"

I am here to tell you that nobody cares!! They don't give two figs about what you do. It's what you will do for them. The only thing anyone wants to know is:

- How are you going to solve my problem?
- Are you the one who can do that?
- And, why should I pick you over all your competition?

In other words, stop selling! When introducing yourself make a connection. Ditch the pitch. Forget canned messages. Rather, seek ways to connect commonalities. Think of the person or group you are presenting to and find a way to connect your message to who they are.

Your 30-Second Introductory Pitch.
What do I offer that my competitors do not offer?

Write down all the ways you provide value to your customers:
1. _____
   _____
2. _____
   _____
3. _____
   _____
4. _____
   _____

What benefits do customers receive from my product or service?
1. _____
   _____
2. _____
   _____
3. _____
   _____
4. _____
   _____

When I first started in business, having to introduce myself literally made a wreck of me. My hands would begin to sweat. My stomach turned into knots. And then, a wise mentor told me the secret. *"Check yourself at the door. Only think about the other people."*

If you want to capture attention, ask a question. Tell a quick story. Listen first before it is your turn and consider how the group responds to each presenter. Your goal is to create a connection, offer a call to action and continue the conversation after the introductions are over.

Remember, people are buying a brighter tomorrow, a better future, a solution to their problems. Use words that have impact, capture attention, paint a brilliant picture. This is not to say use hyperbole. In fact, just the opposite. Instead, be authentic, show you truly care and express why.

Why do you think someone purchases an electric drill? Certainly it's not because the drill is pretty or comes with a carrying case. These attributes might cement the final deal but, first, the buyer has to believe this drill is excellent at making holes! Think benefit, not feature.

When crafting your introductory message keep these tips in mind:
- Make every word count.
- Fit your key message into the statement or question.
- Say what you mean in 15 seconds then expand that to 30 seconds and further to 60 seconds. From there you can create a full-blown presentation.
- Always use the same 15 second sentence first. That way people begin to remember you.

Introductions do not have to be safe – they do have to be creative.

When meeting people 1 on 1, here are some questions you can ask to keep the other person talking. The more information you receive in this first encounter, the better equipped you are to provide just the right solution.
1. Where do you work?
2. What inspired you to go into that field?
3. What do you like most about what you do?
4. What do you like least about what you do?
5. How do you approach the work you do?

Everyone loves to talk about themselves! Think of all you will learn if you get the other person talking. And, another key is, when you really focus in on what the other person is saying, you are able to respond with stories that move the conversation along. For example, in talking with someone who owns a retail boutique I talk about fashion and how I loved going to the dress store with my mother when I was in high school. Soon, the retail owner and I are exchanging childhood stories. Don't be afraid to tell stories.

Common ground is found in storytelling. Storytelling humanizes us. It lets us see who the other person really is. When we exchange stories we get to know each other. We start to build a relationship. If you always look at your introduction as a stepping stone to new relationships, that should make you genuinely interested in the other people in the room. Then your introduction does not sound like a pitch. It doesn't sound canned.

Also be sure your choice of words creates immediate interest for further discussion. That means always include a Call for Action.

In addition to choosing the right words, maintain a professional presence, be upbeat and show genuine interest in the other person. Your choice of words makes all the difference.

- The first 30 seconds are crucial to starting a relationship. People decide in the first 10 seconds if they want to interact with you further. When you open your mouth, choose your words carefully.
- The 30-second introduction is a real game-changer.
- Just as every batter in baseball has to concentrate on what's coming at them, you can never underestimate the power of your pitch. But, unlike baseball, when you pitch, you want to score a home run!

The moral of all this is: Words have Power. Words should inspire Hope. Here is a list of powerful words you can insert into your introduction to increase the value of your proposition.

1. Maximize, increase, grow
2. Minimize, reduce, decrease, eliminate
3. Profit from
4. Specific, specifically
5. Save, conserve
6. Accumulate, acquire
7. Prevent
8. Cut costs
9. Immediate, now

Abraham Lincoln said: *"Better to remain silent and be thought a fool than to speak out and remove all doubt."*

Now, let's see how creative you can get with your pitch. Use these prompts to get you going:
- WHY do you do what you do? (What drives you?)
- WHY should the person or company care? (How will they benefit?)
- WHO are you, anyway? (Why do I want to get to know you better?)

CRAFT YOUR MESSAGE HERE:

1. Why does my business exist? What are we passionate about? _____

_____

_____

2. How do I promote value? How do I make your job easier? _____

_____

_____

3. What problems do I solve for you? _____

_____

_____

> *"Stop selling. Start helping."*
> —Zig Ziglar

CHAPTER FOUR:
TECHNIQUE WINS THE SALE

THE ART OF QUESTIONING

How you ask questions determines whether your prospect will trust you or not. Once you gain their trust, be sure you are talking with the decision maker. Ask who makes decisions for these products or services. If it is not the person you are speaking with, ask to include that person in future meetings. The right questions give you the pertinent information you need to learn about your prospect and create interest in your products/services.

The right questions lead into the buying process. When you're talking with prospects they're also deciding how much confidence, belief, and trust they have in you. These factors determine whether, or not, they will ultimately make the sale. So what are the right questions to ask?

Open-ended questions, period.
These questions are difficult to answer in one or two words and open up a two-way conversation. Open-ended questions begin with: who, what, why, where, and how. Questions that can be answered with a *yes* or *no* should be used when you expect the answer to be yes, to clarify information; to focus the prospect on reaching a decision; and/or to redirect a conversation that has gone off on a tangent.

Questioning Development Strategy:
Prepare a mental list of information you need to make appropriate presentations leading to closing the sale. From this list, develop 10 questions to uncover needs, problems, concerns, etc. These questions must be well thought out, written down and practiced. Relying on a 'whatever-comes-to-mind' questioning approach is unprofessional and more often than not loses business. To get started, try these....

What have you found....?

What has been your experience...?

What do you like about....?

How have you successfully used...?

What would you change about...?

Examples of Open-ended Questions:

- What legal services is your business in need of?
- What issues have surfaced in conjunction with your reorganization?
- What outside help does your reorganization call for?
- Who buys your products/services?
- What are your best selling products?
- What benefits are you offering your employees, along with their salaries?
- What makes you a good employer?
- Who is your target market?
- Who at your company needs to be involved in a purchase of this kind?

Convert each of these closed questions to open-ended ones:

- Do you need legal services in your business? _____
  _____

- Are you ready to invest in outside help coming in to help solve your reorganization issues? _____
  _____

- Does your retail store carry cell phones? _____
  _____

- Have you considered insurance for your employees? _____
  _____

- Do you know of someone who is relocating to Chicago? _____
  _____

- Are you the right person to make a decision about this purchase? _____
  _____

Closed questions result in a yes or no answer that make it difficult for you to continue the conversation. Asking open-ended questions moves the conversation along and promotes rapport.

10 powerful open-ended questions you can ask your prospective clients that will give you the information you need to understand the value you can provide.

1. _____

2._____

3. _____

4. _____

5. _____

6. _____

7. _____

8. _____

9. _____

10. _____

"To find out what your prospects are really thinking, imagine them as onions! Each question you ask is a layer that, when peeled away, gets you closer to the heart of the onion where its strength and power lie. It's easy to interact with people on the most superficial levels, but it keeps you from uncovering the real issues that affect decisions." —Dave Kahle, *Personal Selling Power*

VALUES ALIGNMENT

When talking about your product/service always sell value. And, be sure your personal values are consistent with your professional ones. Very few of us really consider if who we are aligns with our company values.

Answer these 5 questions:

1. Who am I, really? _____

2. What values do I stand for? _____

3. What attitudes do I respect and hire for? _____

4. How do I model these attitudes? _____

5. In what ways does my business reflect what I stand for? _____
   _____

There's a lot of conversation today that confirms when you integrate your personal values into your business, you automatically create stronger teams that live your mission and help drive growth. Think about what it might mean to your business if you align your values vertically and horizontally throughout your company and sell with the same mindset.

FOCUS ON SOLUTIONS

Give prospects reason to buy from you. Focus on the service and benefits of the products/services you offer and get to the emotional need they satisfy. How do the unique features of your products and services address a problem? What solutions do you offer for each?

Problems (description/characteristic)	Solutions (the value your product/service provides)
1.	A.
	B.
	C.
2.	A.
	B.
	C.
3.	A.
	B.
	C.

OVERCOME OBJECTIONS

Many business people resist asking for their prospect's business for one or more of the following reasons:

• Fear of Rejection

That's a natural feeling, but by not asking, you risk losing the business. You need to be proactive during the entire sales process. Think of rejection as one more step closer to making the sale.

- Fear of hidden objections
  This can happen but by not asking you risk losing the business altogether. Somewhere in understanding the prospect's needs, you overlooked some information and emphasized the wrong need.

Every objection gives you an opportunity to get back on track. At this point, you need to be flexible and present a benefit to fit the situation the customer presents.

- Fear of misreading buying cues
  This can happen if you are not attentive to the verbal and non- verbal cues the customer is communicating.

> *"Obstacles don't have to stop you. If you run into a wall, don't turn around and give up. Figure out how to climb it, go through it, or work around it."* —Michael Jordan

List 2 objections you can expect to encounter from a prospect along with an appropriate response.

Objection 1 _____

_____

Response 1 _____

_____

Objection 2 _____

_____

Response 2 _____

_____

ASK FOR THE SALE

There are a variety of ways to ask for the sale, but they all have the same purpose - to allow customers the opportunity to give you their business.

Follow these steps and you will find you start closing more sales.

1. Summarize the customer's need

When you reiterate the need expressed by the customer you open the door to questions that may be unstated. By answering these questions before asking for the business you make sure to remove all objections.

"Mrs. Duncan, you agree that saving money for your children's education is important, and that automatically transferring $100 monthly from your checking account to a college bound fund would make it easy to start investing for your children's education needs."

2. Ask for the business

There are several options you can use, depending on the situation:

- Suggest the logical next step
  "To start this project, all I need is your signature here."

- Give the customer a choice
  "Would either Tuesday or Wednesday afternoon be convenient for you to meet with me to discuss the appropriate machine?"

- Ask for a small commitment
  "Why not start with the moisturizer today and then we can talk about the make-up at a later date. How does that sound to you?"

- Stress a deadline
  "Mr. Roberts, if you order your paper in the next ten days, you can save 20% before the price per ream increases."

- Use an "If-Then' scenario
  "If you commit to the new plan today, you can start saving on all your long-distance calling and have the use of the built-in camera for your son's party."

• Use a form of evidence

"A number of our customers find overdraft protection linked to their checking account beneficial. They saved money because they avoided NSF charges and didn't worry about overdrawing their checking account. If you ever inadvertently overdrew your account, it would be beneficial for you, too, and it would give you peace of mind. Shall I go ahead and set this up for you?"

• Ask the customer to try it

"Why don't you try the telephone PC help line? The next time you have a computer software problem, use the service and see how convenient and easy it is to get your computer up and running. I can set this service up for you in a matter of minutes."

There are numerous ways to ask for the customer's business. No way is any better than another. The important thing is to complete the opportunity you started in the sales process by asking for the customer's business.

> *"The difference between the right word and the almost right word is the difference between lightning and a lightning bug!"* —Mark Twain

CHAPTER FIVE:
DIFFERENTIATE YOUR STYLE

SALES KIT / VISUAL RESOURCES

What sales tools can assist you to motivate prospects to buy your product/ service? What visual resources do you have available in your sales kit? Your sales kit should be accessible via email. If your industry warrants the expenditure you may want printed materials as well.

• Business Cards	• Referrals
• Product/Service Information	• Sample Client List
• Product Sample(s)	• Company Information/Bios
• Pictures	• Press Releases
• Graphs and Charts	• Research Studies
• Testimonials	• Premium give-aways

Visual resources, including digital media, play important roles in supporting your message BUT... your verbal message is the real driving force for the presentation and sale. Visual resources are there to support your message.

To determine which visual resources to use, ask yourself: Is there an element of the product/service that is better portrayed through a visual resource? If so, it belongs in your sales kit. Now determine the best way to package visual resources you'll use:

- Folders
- Binders
- Brochures
- Flip Charts
- Lap-top Presentation
- Videos

All resources should be digital ready.

Before meeting with prospects, select visual resources relevant to your sales objectives. Whichever visual resources are being used, they should focus on helping prospects see how well your product/service satisfies their needs.

PRESENT EFFECTIVE PITCHES

Never jump into making a presentation during the initial interview process. Once you are certain there is interest, these steps will guide your approach.

The next step in selling is becoming so confident in making a presentation that you grab your prospect's interest, create desire and cause action. The success of your presentation either in front of a group or with one person depends not only on your delivery, but also on how listeners perceive your professional image. Research shows people form opinions within two-three seconds of contact. Your appearance, voice, words and mood have an immediate impact on people.

- Appearance

  Create a professional, confident impression in the mind of prospects by appearing neat, and businesslike.

- Tone of voice

  Use a confident, well-controlled tone of voice. If your tone lacks confidence, the benefits of your product/service will lose credence and if your voice is either too loud, too soft, gruff, or harsh, people will stop listening.

- Words

  Be cautious of the words you use. Listeners' demeanor can become defensive if they perceive the words they hear are partronizing or judgemental.

- Mood

  Appear upbeat, enthusiastic, and passionate about your product/service. If you come across as blasé or distracted, you'll have a difficult time selling your ideas to others.

When presenting to a group, use the following checklist to deliver an effective presentation:

- Content

  Follow your agenda keeping in mind the objectives you expect to accomplish from the presentation. No notes are best of all. If you must use notes, make them easy to read. Color-coding points to emphasize helps you to see them quickly.

- Vocal Rate and Tone

  Speak at a rate that will allow the listener to understand what you are saying and/or to take notes without missing your next point. Keep the tone of your voice friendly and confident. If you speak too softly or preachy, you run the risk of losing your listener's interest.

- Audio-visual Equipment and Visual Aids

  Pre-test equipment you are planning to use. If an equipment problem occurs during your presentation, don't waste time trying to get the equipment to work. It's distracting to your listener's comprehension of your message. Instead, always be prepared with a backup plan.

  Visual aids should clarify your message, not be the message itself. All visual aids should be clear, readable, easy to understand, and communicate a single idea.

- Written Material(s)

  Supplementary materials such as brochures are an efficient way to communicate information about your product/service. When passing out materials, allow people to look through them briefly before you start speaking.

- Body Language

  How you stand, movements made with your hands and face, and eye contact engage the prospect with your ideas. Stand or sit firm and erect, smile and mean it, and maintain eye contact, without staring. Use hand gestures to emphasize an idea, but avoid pointing at your listener.

Most of all, have fun. Let your passion shine through. If a presentation doesn't go the way you want, dust yourself off and start all over again. Keep practicing and soon you will be a veteran sales person. Continue to Think Sales and very shortly you will be at the top of your class. As you now know, effective selling can be learned and you have started the process by reading this book.

Here's to you and all the sales you will close!

CHAPTER SIX:
AFTER THE SALE

An entire book could be written on each of the following points. I include them because they are so important to the long-term sustainability of your business. Once you crack the sales code, turn your attention to these key areas.

FOLLOW UP FOR SUCCESS

All too often we forget that the process only really begins after we meet someone for the first time. Don't be in too much of a rush. Your prospect has to get to know you, to feel comfortable doing business with you and to trust that his/her business is safe with you.

During your first meeting, ask your prospect what the best way is to follow up with them. Ask if they would like to meet soon or in 2 months. Be specific. Ask if you should call, email or set up another meeting now? When corresponding, acknowledge that some people prefer LinkedIn to email. If another meeting is not going to happen quickly make sure you stay in touch. Here are some ways to do that:

- Send an article of interest via email.
- Forward articles of interest directly from the source via social media.
- Write a personal thank you note and mail it!
- If you have a newsletter, ask if they wish to receive it.
- Remember special occasions and acknowledge them.
- Offer consultative services.

GO FOR MORE

Too often we concentrate so hard on selling our product/service to our customer that we forget to maximize the sale by asking what other problems concern them. If we can't directly help with those, we can probably refer them to another company that can. We become bigger and more important in our customer's eyes when our concern is to help them with all their challenges. They begin to look to us for answers in all areas of their businesses. If helping your customers is inherent in the way you do business, you will soon find you are providing other products and services to them. Be available, agreeable and actionable and your business will grow. And, amaze them. The element of surprise works wonders in deepening relationships. In addition to a thank you after an initial meeting, or closing a sale, send them something that delights them or came up in conversation and shows how well you listened.

CUSTOMERS RULE

Have you ever found yourself arguing with a customer? In today's climate of YELP, Social Media, Consumer Action groups and other avenues consumers find to express discontent with a business, you, for sure, must maintain an agreeable approach with your clients, helping to solve any issues that arise within 24 hours. Train your staff exactly how to handle complaints. Never leave anything to chance regarding communication with customers. And don't for a minute believe complaints are only relative to companies who conduct business with consumers. No matter where your clients fall, customers hold the ball!

LIFETIME VALUE

It is true that it costs you so much more—in money and time—to acquire a new customer than to retain current ones. Calculate the revenue each customer brings you in a year and multiply that over 10 years. And, what about the referrals you receive from existing customers? If they stopped doing business with you, those referrals might stop. How much would that cost you?

Imagine if we could turn all our customers into 'raving fans' and 'advocates'! One thing I know, it won't happen because you want it to! However, you can create strategies to that will increase the loyalty of your customers.

Start by training your employees to operate in the same way. As nice as you are, it is specific planning that gets you there.

Share stories about top salespeople and how they got there. Encourage your employees to take courses, listen to webinars, network with winners. Hire a coach to work with them. Offer Lunch n' Learns. Be competitive and stay at the top of your game.

The path is clear: When you become a strong sales person and create sales people of all your employees, you will make more money and lead the life you love.

Think Sales and SOAR!

www.ingramcontent.com/pod-product-compliance
Lightning Source LLC
LaVergne TN
LVHW091211080426

835509LV00006B/945